THE
DUFFER'S
GUIDE TO
CRICKET

COLUMBUS BOOKS
LONDON

Other books in the Duffer's series:
The Official Duffer's Rules of Golf (John Noble)
The Official Duffer's Rules of Tennis (Bob Adams)
The Duffer's Guide to Golf: A Second Slice (Gren)
The Duffer's Guide to Rugby (Gren)
The Duffer's Guide to Coarse Fishing (Mike Gordon)
The Duffer's Guide to Greece (Gren)
The Duffer's Guide to Spain (Gren)

Copyright © 1985 Gren of the *South Wales Echo*

First published in Great Britain in 1985 by
Columbus Books
Devonshire House, 29 Elmfield Road, Bromley, Kent BR1 1LT

Printed and bound by Clark Constable,
Edinburgh, London, Melbourne

ISBN 0 86287 175 1

CONTENTS

Introduction

Cricket is one of the great sporting tests of athleticism, character and cunning. Some say it's *the* greatest of all games.

Cricket has held the British Empire together: the sun never sets on the thwack of leather upon willow.

Cricket is beauty combined with grace and skill and can be played by almost everyone. But probably the most wonderful thing of all about cricket is that it confuses Americans.

So read on, duffer, while we joyfully unfold what until now has probably been a confusing mystery to you.

The Game of Cricket

A cricket match consists of two teams of eleven players (or anything up to eleven players in company cricket).

A coin is tossed to give the winner of the call the right either to bat first, or to field first.

The object of the game is to score more runs than your opponents.

The batting side

Two batsmen occupy opposite ends of the wicket. The one receiving the ball is supposed to hit it, and after doing so runs to the opposite end of the wicket. If he manages this without colliding with the other batsman, a run is deemed to have been scored.

If the batsman hits the ball along the ground and over the boundary, four runs are awarded.

If the batsman hits the ball and it crosses the boundary without hitting the ground, six runs are awarded.

It's better to go for the boundary shots – it saves all that undignified running up and down.

7

The fielding side

The prime function of the fielding side is to get the batsmen out. The secondary aim is to stop the batsmen scoring. This can be done by clever bowling, strategic field placing and tying their bootlaces together.

The bowlers have six bowls per over in turn from each end of the wicket. These six balls are called 'overs', because after six balls it's apparent to everyone whether a bowler is 'over the hill'.

There are many ways to get batsmen out: he can be bowled, caught, leg-before-wicket, run out, stumped . . . or you can bribe the umpire to make up something.

The umpires

These gentlemen are out there to ensure fair play. They are men of great integrity, knowledge and dignity who judge the game fairly and fearlessly. Any decision on an appeal for dismissal will be considered honestly and without favour – unless, of course, they are related to the batsman.

Correct Dress

In cricket, great importance is placed upon how well turned-out players are. It's all very well marching on to open the batting with one pad and blue denims if you're playing in some works fun game, but for you or your club to be taken seriously you must dress properly.

The following advice might, therefore, be helpful for duffers.

2. **Sweater:** always wear it, even though it's five sizes too big and the wrong club's colours have been included into it: this will please your doting auntie who knitted it.

1. **Cap:** should be large enough to contain essential equipment — cigarettes, miniatures of Scotch, etc., bottle of Valium. . . .

7. **Shirt:** should ideally be plain white or white-ish. Never wear lilac — it attracts the wrong sort of spectators.

8. **Club badges:** if your club doesn't have a badge, glue on a beer-bottle label — it always looks impressive.

3. **Batting gloves:** insist your club supplies them; they're useful for keeping hands warm when washing your car on a chilly winter Sunday morning.

9. **Protective box:** not so much because of what it can do for you but because of what the ladies in the tea room say if you don't think you need one.

4. **Bat:** useful for fending off any ball that comes near you, and for attacking Australian fans who invade the wicket areas.

10. **Easily understood markings:** there's nothing worse than thinking you're playing off your front foot or sweeping to leg when you're not sure of your left foot from your right. Always mark things clearly.

5. **Pads:** these keep your legs warm and are very useful when scrubbing floors.

11. **Cricket boots:** for village or company cricket whitened football boots will do.

6. **Trousers:** white (with red stains for bowlers). Pockets should be large enough to accommodate smuggled sausage rolls from the tea room.

LEG

OFF

BACK FOOT

FRONT FOOT

11

Types of Cricketer

Cricket is a game of specialist skills. The players are selected for their abilities in certain areas, e.g. batting, bowling or fielding. Players who do all things equally badly are called all-rounders.

The batsman

These are players who are in the team because their concentration, speed of eye and reaction to the ball enables them to despatch it with uncanny accuracy to pre-selected parts of the boundary, missing lurking fielders with pin-point precision – now and then.

If batsmen miss a ball, they pretend to have left it alone on purpose. If the ball hits the wicket, quick-thinking batsmen of course claim that a no-ball had been called.

The bowler

These come in two types:

(a) The fast bowler

A nasty, aggressive type who takes great delight in hurling the ball at the poor batsman in the hope of giving him a nasty body blow; failing that, he'd even settle for his hurled missile hitting the stumps. Duffers should avoid fast bowlers at all costs.

(b) The spin bowler

Spin bowlers are either former fast bowlers who have developed cartilage problems or batsmen who are having a rough season with the bat. Duffers should always try to play against spin bowlers. It's less painful.

The fielder

The specialist fielder, hoping he looks cat-like, pounces on a snicked ball in a flash, making batsmen scurry back to the safety of the crease. Specialist fielders are usually found at first slip, where their incredible reactions ensure they dive and just fail to hold a ball which, had it not been fumbled, would have carried to second slip for a simple catch.

Duffers should remember it is nobler to be a specialist batsman who fields a bit than to be a specialist fielder who bats a bit.

The wicket keeper

He is unmistakable. He is the one wearing legpads but not carrying a bat.

Wicket keepers shout ' 'Owzat?' at every other ball, dive around a lot and generally make nuisances of themselves.

They hide directly behind batsmen to confuse slow bowlers, yet if a big, nasty fast bowler is hurling them down, they stand as far away as possible.

Wicket keepers are extroverts with at least two false teeth.

The all-rounder

The all-rounder bats, fields and bowls equally badly. When his batting is worse than usual, he pretends to be concentrating on his bowling and vice versa. When his bowling and batting are both off, he explains that he's slipped a disc while performing miracles at forward short leg. Duffers should always offer themselves to their selected club as an all-rounder. They'll welcome you with open arms and it'll take months for them to discover you can't do anything well, by which time you should have engineered a blackmail hold over the captain.

Types of Cricket

As an innocent duffer, you probably thought that all cricket is just cricket. Nothing is ever that simple, of course. Even this, the most civilized of games, has at least five variations of its basic game groups.

1. Test cricket

This is the very top flight of cricket: world-class players representing their countries, pitting their combined skills against one another in a contest which can take up to five days to complete – and, sometimes, even then fails to conclude.

Test tours are always cleverly timed to ensure that the touring party is able to miss the winter at home (some established players haven't seen snow for ten years).

The British test team is called the England XI, which is a good thing for all Welsh, Irish and Scots because they seem to lose a lot.

2. County cricket

These are the teams from which the test squad is selected. County players used to be men of the county who proudly represented their area. Nowadays, county teams are full of overseas players, mercenaries, sons of businessmen who have easily withdrawable financial stakes in the club. Some players are even selected because they make good after-dinner speeches.

You can almost always spot the county players – they're the ones who speak in an accent foreign to that of the county.

This doesn't, however, apply to Yorkshire CCC. They all have local accents, as you will hear if ever you get close enough to hear them quarrelling with one another.

3. League cricket

This is a very high standard of cricket. The teams are made up of players who would be ashamed to say they were county players. Others in the league team have been dismissed by the county for fraud, drunkenness, bawdy behaviour or behaving in a tired and emotional manner with the county president's wife.

Generally, a good crowd, whose company the duffer will enjoy.

4. Company cricket

This is cricket played between teams made up of decrepit office and factory workers, all of whom are at least fifteen years past their prime – assuming they ever had a prime. They turn up late, usually at the wrong park's pitch, on Wednesdays and Saturdays, to do battle with the opposition of – on a good day – eleven.
The progress of the game must never interfere with getting to the pub, wherein the players exaggerate the ability they possessed in former years, before it closes.
Company cricketers are fun to be with. The duffer should aim to play badly enough to be included in such a side.

5. Village cricket

The greatest of all cricket. The true meaning of cricket. The purest form of cricket. It goes without saying that to get the best out of village cricket, one should live in the village. The team is made up of locals: the local bank manager, the local vicar, the local farmer, the local doctor, the local pervert, and so on.

Real village cricket has to be played on a real village green, while spectators spectate from a field-side pub with a thatched roof.

If you, the duffer, ever find such a place, move to the village and never ever roam. It's a sort of heaven on earth.

Batting Strokes

Whether, as a duffer, you wish to understand the game as a spectator or actually to take part, it's important to realize that when the chappie with the lump of wood (the bat) is out there in the middle (the wicket) of the field (the middle), he isn't just clouting everything or even trying to clout everything in the same way.

There are varying styles of delivery from the bowler, and the man holding the lump of wood (the batsman) has to vary his strokes to suit.

1. Playing off the front foot

Batsmen, unlike normal people (who have two feet dangling side by side), have a front foot and a back foot.

The front foot is, for a right-handed batsman, his left foot — and, for a left-handed batsman, his right foot.

It is therefore very important that the aspiring batsman should know whether he is right- or left-handed. If he can't tell, he should ask someone in the scorers' box. Sometimes they can tell.

A real duffer, however, would never play off the front foot.

25

2. Playing off the back foot

In back-foot play, the batsman hopes to get as far away from the bowler as possible – without actually standing on the wrong side of the wicket, which can be effective but upsets wicket keepers.

3. The off-drive

This is the classic shot in which the ball is despatched to an area on the left of the bowler and to your right – assuming you're a normal, right-handed person.

If, however, the ball goes to the right of the bowler, you will, of course, claim intent and accept congratulations for an on-drive.

4. The sweep

If you are unfortunate enough to fall while trying to smash a ball to leg, you can, with practice, like most county players, fall with dignity on to one knee only. This disguises the fact that, due to poor timing, footwork and reaction, you fluffed a very easy shot. You will instead be thought to have been brave enough to try to execute the sweep shot.

Duffers sometimes even manage a sweep back to the bowler, wicket keeper, and sometimes even the slips.

5. The hook

This isn't so much a batting stroke as an act of self-defence – usually against a bouncer or a high, full toss from a bowling duffer.

The ball, on line for the throat, is intercepted and fended off by any part of the bat in the interests of continuing to breathe. If a run comes from it too, that's a bonus!

Duffers should use this shot often. Survival instincts ensure it comes naturally.

6. The cut

This is a delightful offside shot which happens when you fail to remove your dangling bat from a ball outside the off stump which accidentally hits the bat and goes speeding to the boundary. Duffers should leave this shot to professionals – or even test players.

7. The clout

The most glorious of all the shots – don't worry about the textbooks, where your feet are or your shoulder is, pointing towards the ball. Just grab the bat at the top of the handle, close your eyes and swing.

If you connect with the ball, you're a hero. If you miss, you're an irresponsible fool and a liability to the side. Still, it's great fun.

Bowling

Bowlers take their craft very seriously and are very sensitive to criticism. We who are not bowlers realize, of course, that they just run up and sling it down, having no control whatsoever over what happens to the ball except for its speed of travel (or lack of it), but, even so, we humour them in their little beliefs that they can make it pop up, swing out, swing in, etc.

The following are some of the types of ball reactions bowlers (and the Test Match Special commentators on radio) think bowlers are able to achieve.

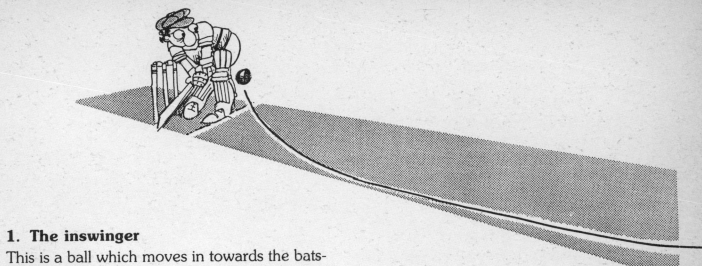

1. The inswinger

This is a ball which moves in towards the batsman because the bowler hasn't concentrated on
swinging his arm properly or has made a hash of
his run-up.

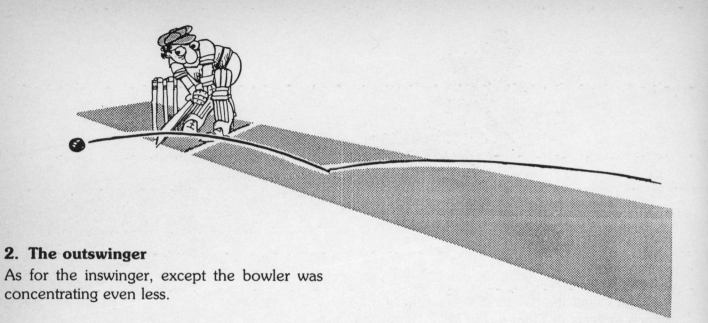

2. The outswinger

As for the inswinger, except the bowler was concentrating even less.

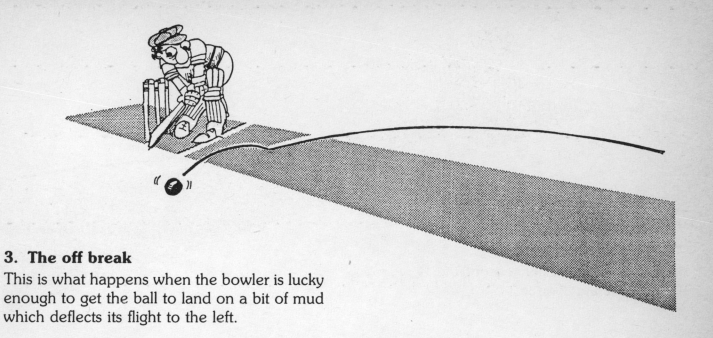

3. The off break

This is what happens when the bowler is lucky enough to get the ball to land on a bit of mud which deflects its flight to the left.

4. The leg break

This occurs when the ball hits the same bit of
mud but goes right.

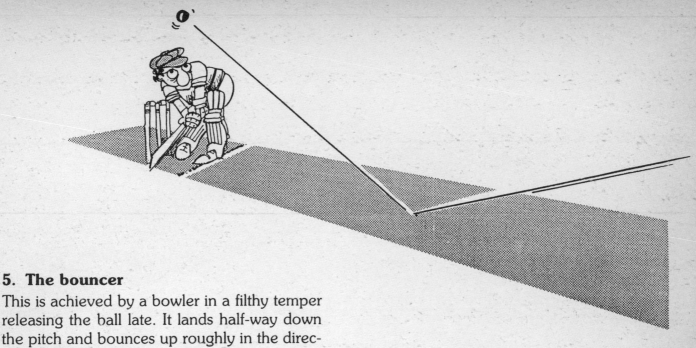

5. The bouncer

This is achieved by a bowler in a filthy temper releasing the ball late. It lands half-way down the pitch and bounces up roughly in the direction of the batsman.

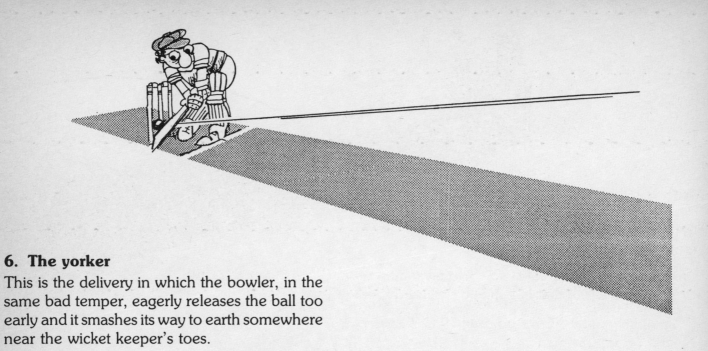

6. The yorker

This is the delivery in which the bowler, in the same bad temper, eagerly releases the ball too early and it smashes its way to earth somewhere near the wicket keeper's toes.

7. The googly

This is what the Test Match Special commentators call a ball that has totally confused them.

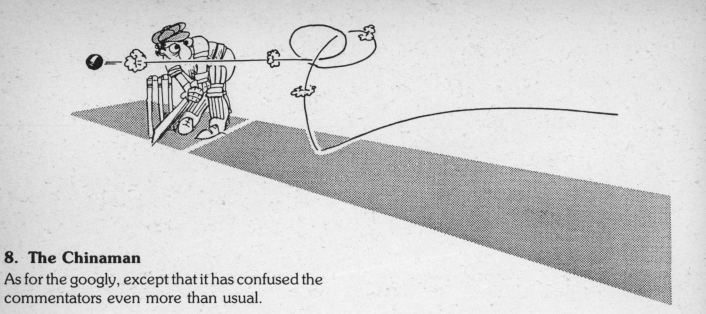

8. The Chinaman

As for the googly, except that it has confused the commentators even more than usual.

Spot the Fielder

While watching a game where, after 150 overs, the score has rattled along to twenty-nine for no wicket and the local beer's rubbish too, duffers may be excused for thinking that cricket is perhaps a trifle unexciting.

Should you find yourself in this situation, do as radio and TV commentators have done over the years: look around the field and play spot-the-character. It helps to pass the time.

1. The womanizer

This chap has slipped the captain a tenner to ensure he fields on the boundary all season. From this position he chats up every lady spectator who is attracted to his sporty image.

When the ball crosses the boundary (as happens frequently) he dives after it, not returning to the field of play until he has at least one lady's 'phone number – sometimes even her address and photograph, too. If his luck's really in, he may be smothered in lipstick as well.

The womanizer is usually a sales rep.

2. The I-don't-give-a-damn type

This chap is usually from Yorkshire and thinks, therefore, that he can play a bit and, to complete the image, ought to be a bit gruff and rude. He never turns up for practice, but presents his scruffy presence for each game, where he loudly appeals for everything and afterwards drinks more than anyone else in either team.

This type is usually a plumber or a welder.

3. The flashy

Likes to field near the bat so that he can show off – diving, cartwheeling, jumping, and throwing his body acrobatically at any ball within fifteen feet of him.

Best of all he likes to spring after a ball that has eluded his grasp, hoping to overtake it – sometimes he even throws his cap at it – before finally making a theatrical dive at it as the ball limps over the boundary.

Keen observers of the game will note that this type is very often something in advertising.

4. Bossy boots

This one delights in sending players, with a wag of his authoritative finger, from positions on the leg to positions on the off, or pedantically demanding a sideways alteration of a yard by some poor chap fielding on the boundary.

This type is usually a trades union official playing to relax between strike meetings.

5. The quietly confident

This one is very undemonstrative. Silently, and with a casual air, he waits for over after over until a catching chance comes his way, on which he pounces and, incredibly, holds. Then he throws the ball back to the bowler with an air of 'You didn't think I'd drop it, did you?' as he graciously accepts the congratulations of his amazed colleagues.

This type is usually a theological student or even a vicar.

6. The poseur

Pathetically overpowering as he parades himself in county cap, university scarf, touring blazer over regimental sweater (all second-hand), awaiting the call, the poseur is ever eager to be allowed on, just once – so that he can say he's actually played.

This type is usually a teacher or a defrocked dentist.

47

7. The psychopath

The psychopath is usually a fast bowler who thinks he's licensed to maim. He hurls down deliveries and if they are struck for four or six he becomes more agitated and aggressive.

When, between each over, he is not able to bowl, he delights in trying for run-outs, where in one movement he can stop a well-struck ball and hurl it at the head of one of the batsmen.

The team psychopath is usually a policeman or probation officer.

Umpires' Signals

Even if you are new to the game, you will probably have noticed two gentlemen in white coats out there in the middle of the field. These are not twitching ice-cream sellers. These are umpires. They are there to ensure fair play and the twitching is a series of complex signals designed to convey messages to interested parties such as scorers, spectators and especially radio commentators, to indicate what's happening during the proceedings.

To increase your enjoyment of the game, we offer the following explanations of what the signals mean.

1. I have got cramp in my
   left leg.

2. I have got cramp in my
   right leg.

3. You should have seen
   the one that got away.

4. I am turning right.

5. I've dropped my contact lens.

6. Out!

7. Maybe he's out.

8. I know he's out, but blood is thicker than water.

9. Isn't that Concorde?

10. I didn't see that – I'd nodded off for a moment.

11. I should never have had those curried eggs for lunch.

12. Does anyone know how many balls are left in this over?

13. I've got a verruca.

14. I was unsighted by that tall Australian with the big feet.

15. Don't ask me, I'm too drunk to care.

Field Placings

If cricket holds an even greater joy than seeing Americans confused by it, it's the pure delight of being allowed to place your field – sending duffer players to vague parts of the ground that you describe by name only, while the fielder, not wishing to appear unknowledgeable about the game, will wander off happily bewildered while you continue your orders. 'Fred! Short third fine gully on the leg'; 'Wally, I want you at extra silly and third man cover'. 'Bert, on my googly I want you finer and backward of fifth slip', etc., etc. You can go on for hours like this until one of the more intelligent players twigs you're a lunatic –but until then, it's great fun. Try it as soon as you get the chance.

1. Third man.
2. Deep fine leg.
3. Long leg.
4. Backward point.
5. Second slip.

6. Wicket keeper.
7. Short fine leg or leg slip.
8. Square leg.
9. Umpires.
10. Gully.
11. First slip.
12. Cover point.
13. Short extra cover.
14. Silly mid-off.
15. Forward short leg or silly mid-on.

16. Extra cover.
17. Mid-off.
18. Bowler
19. Mid-on.
20. Mid-wicket.
21. Long-off.
22. Long-on.
23. Almost mid-wicket.
24. Ice-cream salesman.
25. Deep long straight lurker.
26. Wicket keeper's friend.

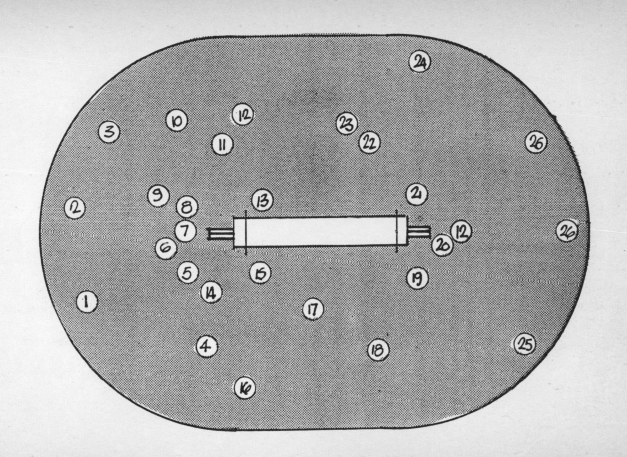

I Play Cricket Because...

The cricket duffer must not believe that love of the game has anything to do with why people play it. Go on, ask any team member to give you an honest answer to 'Why do you play cricket?' None of the answers ever has anything to do with sporting conflict.

1. I just adore dressing up in white, darling.

2. I hate cricket – but it gets
me away from gardening. I
hate that even more.

3. I love inflicting pain and suffering on poncy batsmen – it gives me a sort of warm glow inside and my psychiatrist says it's good for me.

4. I fancy one of the birds
on the ladies' committee.

5. I just love giving a quick hug to anyone who takes a wicket – even sometimes when they don't.

6. I'm the local vicar. I like the community to see me partaking of worldly pleasures.

7. I'd do anything to get
away from the wife and kids.

8. It gets rid of my aggressions.

9. They have great booze-ups after each game.

10. I just love being in the showers with the chaps.

11. I'm the local bank manager and, as the club is into us for £10,000, I like to keep an eye on things.

Cricket Club People

If any duffer should be contemplating joining his local cricket club, he would be well advised to recognize certain cricket club people and keep them at a safe distance. They should only be engaged in conversation when favours are required, e.g. a drink or their supporting vote when he stands for committee office.

The following are the types common to all clubs. Duffers, you have been warned.

1. The club chairman

He'll never be able to remember your name or what you do within the club. He's vaguely friendly but never sure why, and never sure where the Firsts are playing on Saturday or whether the Seconds have a game at all. Yet he can remember names to drop: 'Compton was a great friend of mine – could never read my wrong 'un, y'know.'

2. The club bore

Avoid this one at all costs, otherwise he'll smother you with reminiscences. His conversation always begins with something like, 'I see Kapil Dev got his hundred before lunch in a bad light against the west zone in Madras yesterday'. Then he drones on about how so-and-so was the best player of a late turner he'd ever seen. He also knows for a fact that the test selectors will never consider so-and-so because of a hushed-up late-night fracas in a Leeds club which involved the wife of an MCC Committee member.

3. The club secretary

There's nothing the club secretary likes as much as little bits of paper, which he fishes out from deep in faded jacket pockets to pin on notice-boards or give to members, advising them of selections, AGMs, duty rotas – sometimes even about the next game.

The secretary will also readily turn out for the team whenever they are short. You can always tell the secretary when he's playing – he's the one who shouts, 'Through the chair, of course, I'd like to ask 'OWZAT?'

4. The club statistician

With his breast pocket full of pens and pencils, the club statistician is a real pain. When you're holding forth about the best performance you've ever seen by anyone in this club, he'll cleverly remind you that in the summer of '47 someone scored more, or faster, or with fewer strokes or with less players on the leg.

The statistician will collect boringly useless details which will never be used – except to make you look a fool next time you offer an opinion. Remember the old adage – always distrust people who have a breast pocket full of pens and pencils.

5. The tea ladies

The tea ladies are little treasures, twittering away their afternoons as they delicately slice sandwiches, put little sticks through bits of cheese and make gallons of tea.

Many a tea lady has had marriage proposed to her by an impressed club player, just on the strength of her sandwich-making.

Tea ladies must be treated with great respect and affection by the duffer. They could ruin your cricketing career just by the offering of a dodgy prawn open sandwich.

Commentators' Jargon

Radio cricket commentators are a very special breed, forever worrying about statistics and silly questions, such as 'Who was the last man to score a century at Lords when there was a left-handed scoreboard operator on and one of the umpires was a Baptist?' To shut them up during test matches, listeners even send cakes up to the commentary box – but that doesn't work, either. 'When was the last time a Black Forest gâteau arrived before tea on the third day while Botham was on at the pavilion end?'

Even so, they have a difficult job to do – unlike us, they can't hurl abuse at the players from the safety of the stands. They have to make do with snide remarks thinly disguised as descriptions of play, but we who have spent many years listening to their prattle know what they really mean, don't we?

He sometimes sacrifices accuracy for extra pace.
If he gets one on the wicket, Lord help the batsman.

He thinks deeply about the game.
He gets maudlin when he's drunk.

He can certainly motivate his team.
He's the big-mouth of the side.

**There are those who
say he should be
in the England team.**
His mother said so
last night.

**You've got to admire
him — always trying
something new.**
You don't often see
donkey drops at
this level of
cricket.

**He really is a leg-
spinner with a
difference.**
He can't make
any ball turn.

He's tied the batsman down for some time.
He hasn't managed to get a single ball on the wicket for the last ten overs.

His field placing is interesting.
I haven't got a clue what he's playing at.

The umpire's interpretation of that law was interesting.
The one-eyed twit missed that again!

79

**His father used to play
that shot a lot, I remember.**
He was rubbish, too.

**He won the toss and
boldly gambled on
putting them in to bat
on this good wicket.**
He's a pratt.